WHERE'S WALLY?
ACROSS LANDS

MARTIN HANDFORD

WALKER BOOKS
AND SUBSIDIARIES
LONDON · BOSTON · SYDNEY · AUCKLAND

WIZARD
WHITEBEARD

WALLY

ODLAW

WENDA

WOOF

HI, WALLY FANS,

JOIN ME ON A HOTFOOT-IT HIKE TO FAR, FAR AWAY LANDS! AMBLE ACROSS ANCIENT CITIES, ROAM DEEP, DARK CAVES AND SCALE CASTLE WALLS! ALSO MEET CLEVER CLANS OF PEOPLE AND SOME MISCHIEVOUS MONSTERS!

NOW, HERE COMES THE CHALLENGE ... CAN YOU SOLVE THE PUZZLING PUZZLES ALONG THE WAY? WOW! WHAT AN ADVENTURE! AND DON'T FORGET TO SEARCH NORTH, SOUTH, EAST AND WEST OF THESE PAGES FOR A PRECIOUS GEM.

BY THE WAY, I'M NOT TRAVELLING ON MY OWN. WHEREVER I GO, WOOF, WENDA, WIZARD WHITEBEARD AND ODLAW GO TOO. SEE IF YOU CAN TRACK DOWN OUR LOST THINGS AS WE WANDER HERE, THERE, EVERYWHERE AND ANYWHERE!

| WALLY'S KEY | WOOF'S BONE | WENDA'S CAMERA | WIZARD WHITEBEARD'S SCROLL | ODLAW'S BINOCULARS |

COMPASSES AND MAPS OUT, DEAR FRIENDS! HAVE FUN!

Wally

GREAT GUIDEBOOKS

Off we go! Strike through ten books that the riddles rule out to reveal the one I'm taking on my travels.

STONE AGE ART

Animal Antics

The book you're looking for…

* Has no shields or swords…
* Or anything made of bricks or stone.
* It's not about four-legged creatures.
* No cameras are allowed.
* Its travel tips go beyond the globe.
* It's full of mysteries, but they are not golden.
* Its route may (or may not!) take you north, south, east or west.

HOW TO TAME A MONSTER

The Secrets of Ancient Gold

THE LAST DAYS OF THE AZTECS

TRAVELLING THE WORLD

ANCIENT ROME

THE RIDDLE OF THE PYRAMIDS

WENDA'S PHOTOGRAPHY GUIDE

At the Castle

ODLAW'S SNEAKY DIRECTIONS

MORE THINGS TO DO

* Keep your eyes peeled for lands that Wally travels to where some of these great guidebooks might be useful.

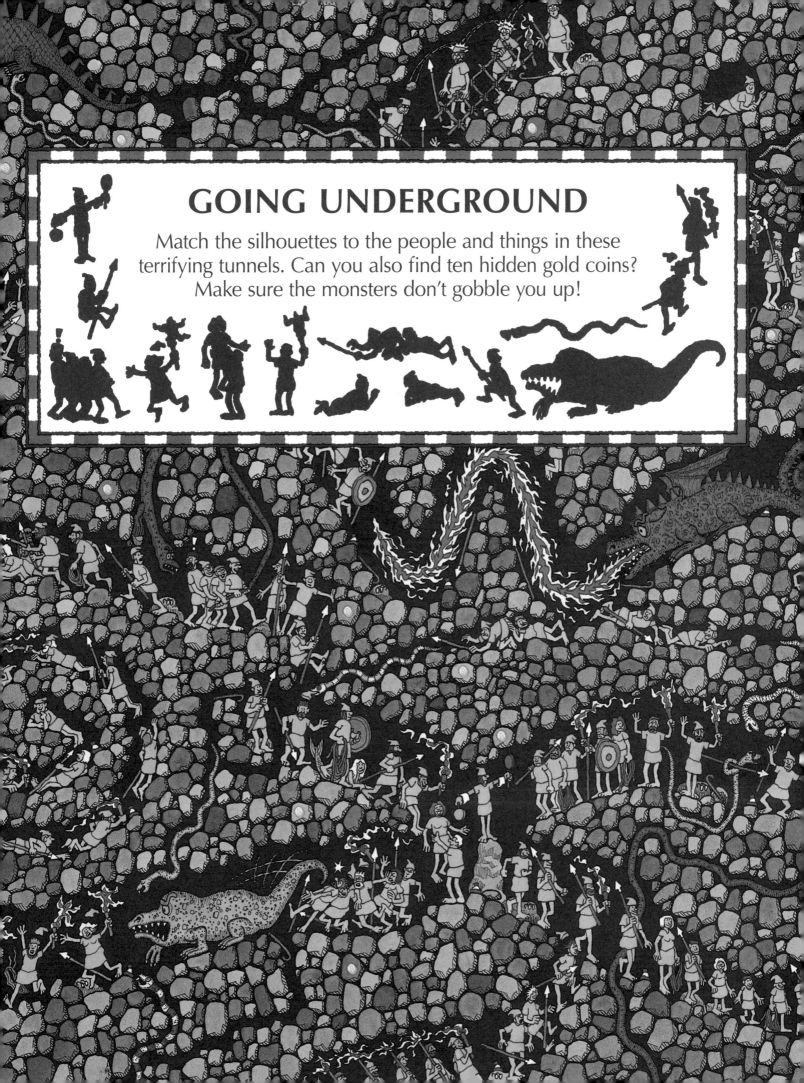

GOING UNDERGROUND

Match the silhouettes to the people and things in these
terrifying tunnels. Can you also find ten hidden gold coins?
Make sure the monsters don't gobble you up!

THE TERRIFIC TEMPLE TREK

Follow my journey through Mexico until you find the
secret hiding place of the Aztec gold hoard.

❶ **Start your journey** by finding a Spanish Conquistador holding
a flag with a double-headed eagle on it. ❷ **Walk along** the base of
the pyramid and climb up the tower of soldiers until you reach the man
with the very tall red-and-orange feather headdress. Careful not to get
hit on the head! ❸ **Climb over** to the stairs at his right and run up to the
platform at the top. Greet the man wearing the four large feathers.

❹ **Slide down** the right-hand side of the stairs. Once you get past the falling rock, see if you can find the man with closed eyes holding a crossbow in one hand. ❺ **At ground level** walk to the right and find an Aztec warrior holding a yellow-and-black stripy shield. Do you think he knows Odlaw?
❻ **Crawl over** to a dropped yellow-and-black stripy shield. Avoid the falling man! ❼ **Jump onto** the grey horse and let the helmeted rider trot you round the corner. ❽ **Tip-toe up** the stairs to the top.
❾ **Dash into** the open mouth without being seen!

MORE THINGS TO FIND

- [ ] Nine birds
- [ ] Twenty-eight shields with feathers
- [ ] A man with his fingers in his ears
- [ ] Three men wearing gold medallions
- [ ] A pickpocket
- [ ] Eight men in yellow costumes with black spots

SURVIVAL SEQUENCES

Study the order of the pictures in the example, then fill in the blanks in games 1, 2 and 3. (The sequence starts over again when it reaches the end symbol.)

EXAMPLE

GAME 1

GAME 2

GAME 3

MORE THINGS TO DO

* Draw your own stick man sequence!

CAVE LIFE QUIZ

We stumbled upon amazing caves! Here are questions to bamboozle your brain, some have more than one answer!

1. The Stone Age is called the Stone Age because…
- [ ] Tools were made of stone
- [ ] Beds were made of rocks
- [ ] Dinosaurs threw stones

2. During this time, the people…
- [ ] Hunted and gathered food
- [ ] Didn't hunt for food
- [ ] Got takeaway food

3. Found on cave walls were…
- [ ] Paintings of animals
- [ ] Magic doors
- [ ] Paintings of dragons

4. Found in caves were…
- [ ] Bears
- [ ] Baboons
- [ ] Lions

5. Mastodons looked like…
- [ ] Elephants
- [ ] Mice
- [ ] Dogs

6. These things were woolly:
- [ ] Rhinos
- [ ] Mammoths
- [ ] Fish

7. Cavemen knew how to make…
- [ ] Fire
- [ ] Origami
- [ ] Lasagna

8. Wild boar is an ancestor of a…
- [ ] Platypus
- [ ] Porcupine
- [ ] Pig

9. Animal skin and bones were used to make…
- [ ] Clothes
- [ ] Tools
- [ ] Washing-up liquid

10. Handmade tools included…
- [ ] Shields
- [ ] Spears
- [ ] Swords

MORE THINGS TO FIND
- [ ] Two red apples
- [ ] Ten cave dogs
- [ ] Two cave bears

FOOTSTEP FINDS

Start on a character square and follow their footstep guide left to right to find out who wandered where.

MORE THINGS TO FIND

Who landed by a…

- [ ] cake;
- [ ] spooky doorway;
- [ ] man with ticklish feet;
- [ ] hole in the ground;
- [ ] stone statue?

BUILDING BLOCKS

It's crazy and cryptic construction time! Can you complete each grid using only the shaped blocks shown underneath it?

HINT: If you get stuck, copy the pieces onto grid paper and cut them out to try different combinations until you get it right!

MORE THINGS TO DO
* Colour in the blocks once you've worked out the answers!

SPECTATOR SPORT

Can you match each person and object in the central, sandy arena with one or more identical copies to reveal the odd one out?

MORE THINGS TO DO

* Draw sandals on some of the Romans' bare feet!

* Think up lion, leopard and tiger taming tricks!

SCALING LADDERS

Fill in the missing words! Start at the top and change only one letter at a time (the rest of the letters stay in the same order).

WALL

_ _ _ _

_ _ _ _

FEEL

BOTTLE

_ _ _ _ _ _

_ _ _ _ _ _

_ _ _ _ T L E

See page 10 and 20 for a clue to the word above!

MORE THINGS TO FIND

- ☐ A ladder with eleven rungs
- ☐ Two stripy shields
- ☐ Three cats

MONSTER MAYHEM

Yikes! Helmeted hunters are lost in a monstrous land!
What do you think they are saying, dreaming, singing or yelling?

RIGHT-ANGLED ANIMALS

What creatures lurk in this fantastic forest? Trace and cut up the shaped pieces below and use them to make the animals on the opposite page.

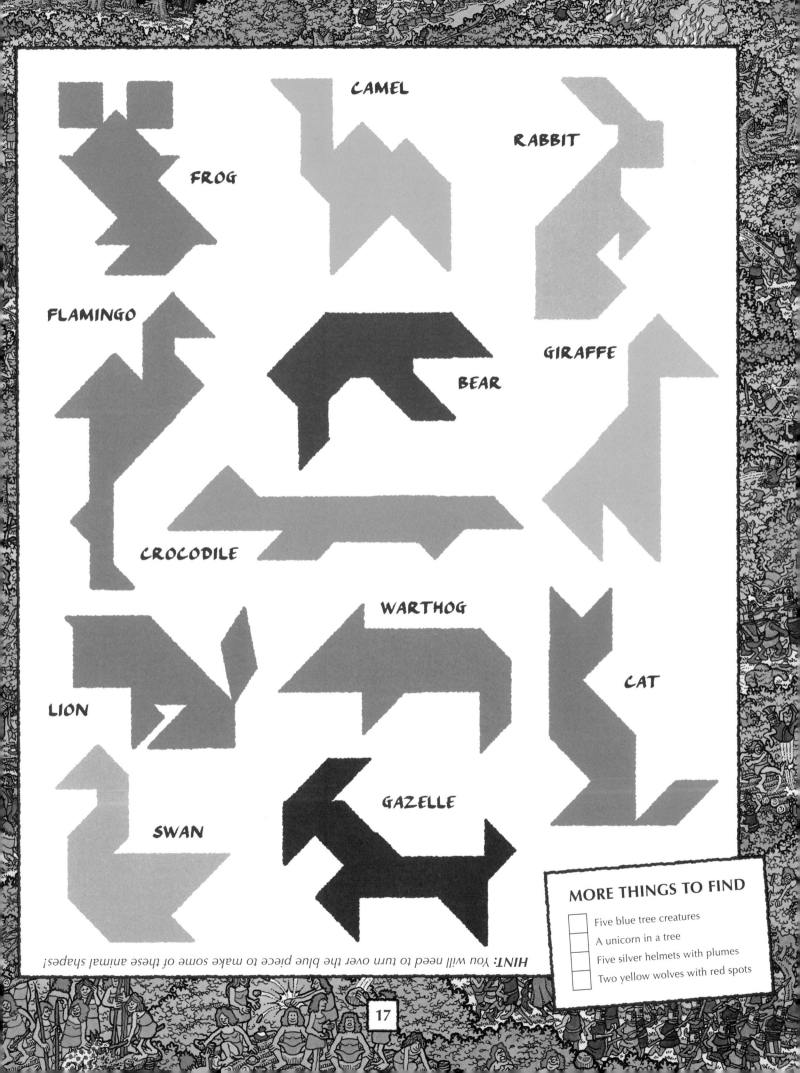

CAMEL

RABBIT

FROG

FLAMINGO

BEAR

GIRAFFE

CROCODILE

WARTHOG

CAT

LION

GAZELLE

SWAN

HINT: You will need to turn over the blue piece to make some of these animal shapes!

MORE THINGS TO FIND

☐ Five blue tree creatures
☐ A unicorn in a tree
☐ Five silver helmets with plumes
☐ Two yellow wolves with red spots

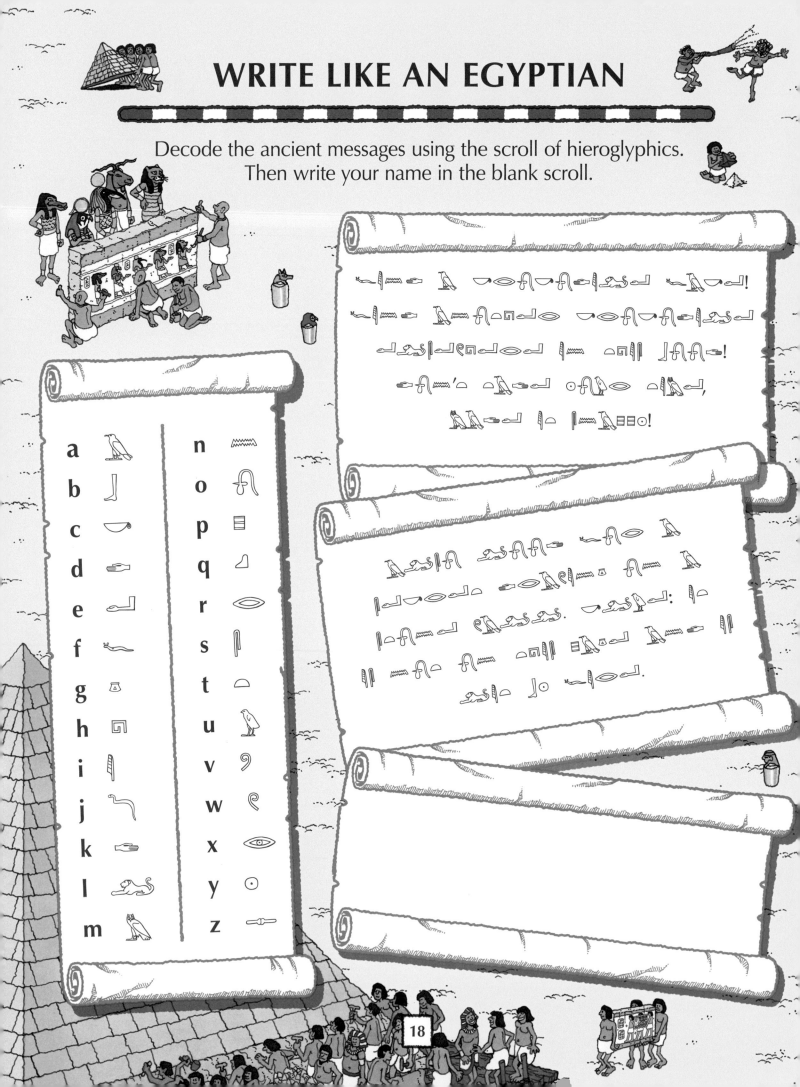

WRITE LIKE AN EGYPTIAN

Decode the ancient messages using the scroll of hieroglyphics.
Then write your name in the blank scroll.

IMAGINE YOUR CITY!

Use the triangles as a guide to build and colour in your very own Egyptian city, just like magic!

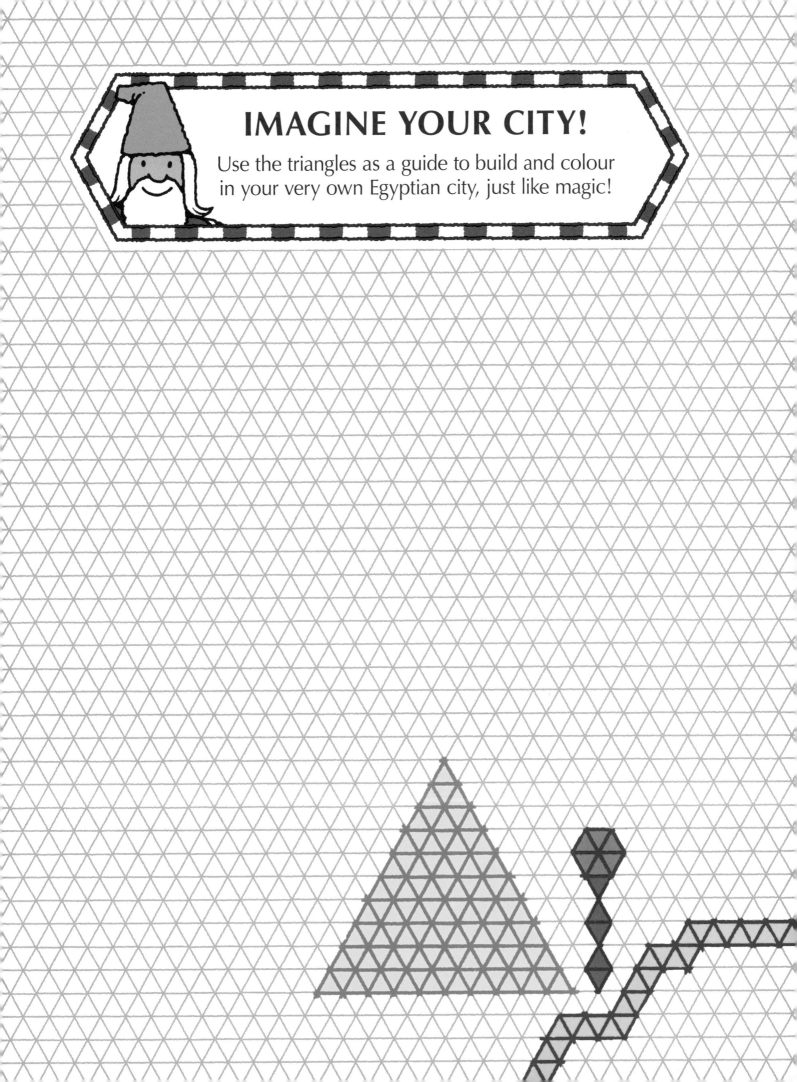

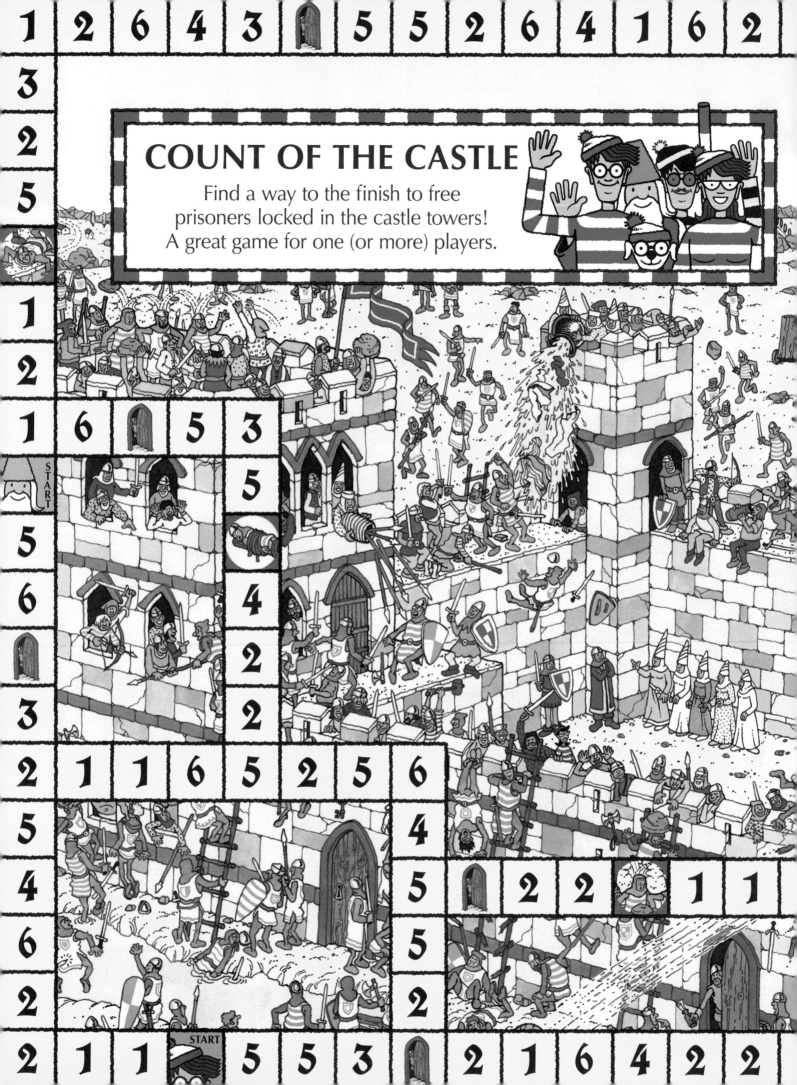

COUNT OF THE CASTLE

Find a way to the finish to free
prisoners locked in the castle towers!
A great game for one (or more) players.

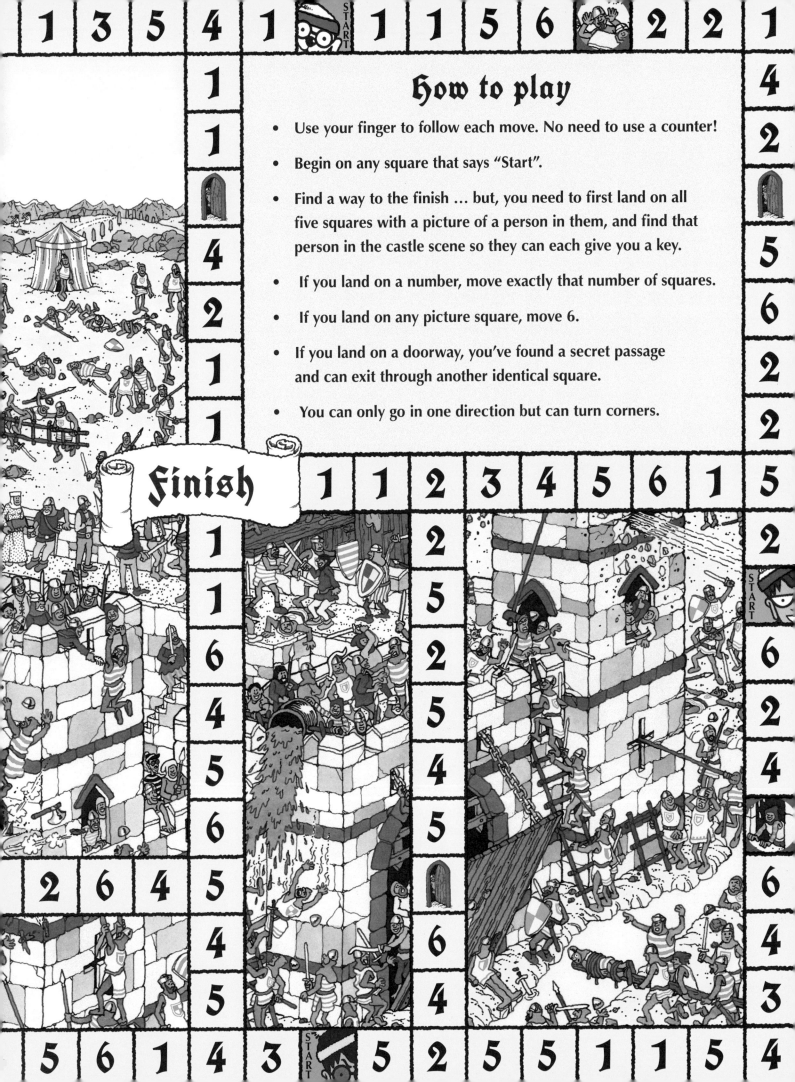

How to play

- Use your finger to follow each move. No need to use a counter!

- Begin on any square that says "Start".

- Find a way to the finish … but, you need to first land on all five squares with a picture of a person in them, and find that person in the castle scene so they can each give you a key.

- If you land on a number, move exactly that number of squares.

- If you land on any picture square, move 6.

- If you land on a doorway, you've found a secret passage and can exit through another identical square.

- You can only go in one direction but can turn corners.

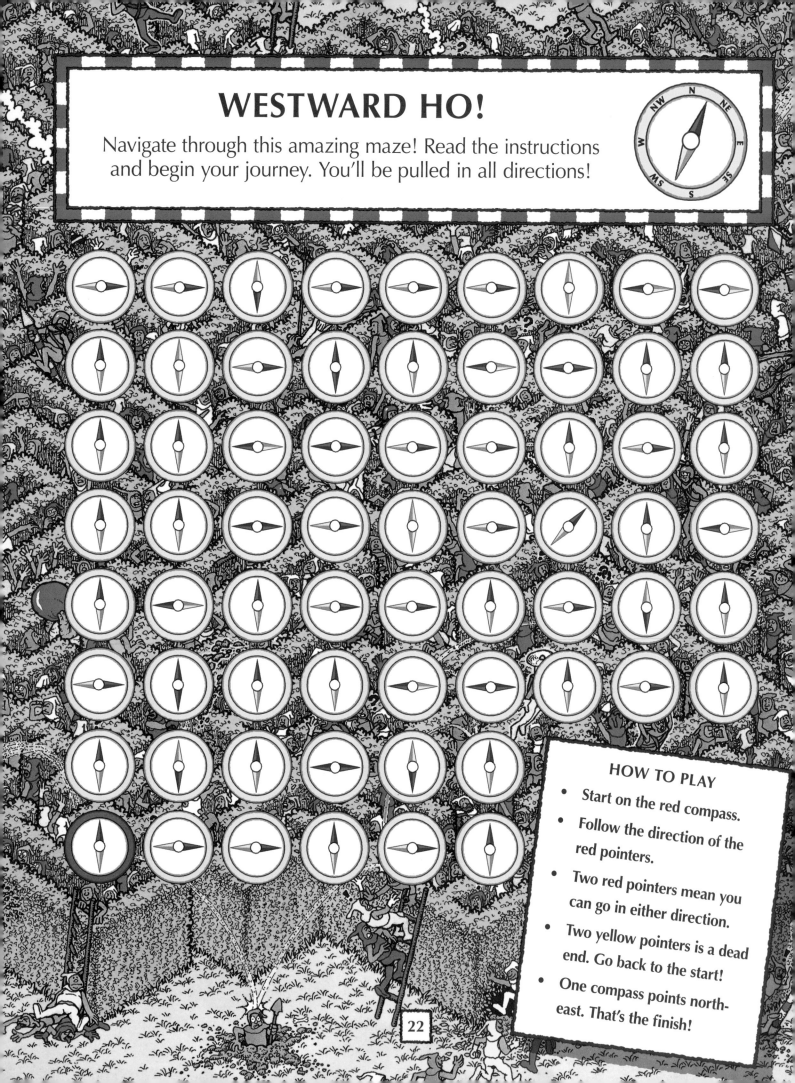

WESTWARD HO!

Navigate through this amazing maze! Read the instructions and begin your journey. You'll be pulled in all directions!

HOW TO PLAY

- Start on the red compass.
- Follow the direction of the red pointers.
- Two red pointers mean you can go in either direction.
- Two yellow pointers is a dead end. Go back to the start!
- One compass points north-east. That's the finish!

WELL DONE, WALLY-WATCHERS! DID YOU FIND THE GREAT GEM TREASURE? IF NOT, THERE'S STILL TIME TO SEARCH FOR IT!

WAIT, THERE'S MORE! LOOK BACK THROUGH THE PICTURES TO FIND THE ITEMS ON THE CHECKLIST AND SHOWN IN THE STRIPY CIRCLES BELOW. IT'S TIME TO HOP, SKIP AND JUMP YOUR WAY BACK TO THE BEGINNING!

Wally

ACROSS LANDS CHECKLIST

- [ ] A sitar player
- [ ] Five trees with faces
- [ ] A message in a bottle
- [ ] Five fair maidens in a line
- [ ] A landscape painting
- [ ] Four broken ladders
- [ ] A green dragon
- [ ] Three muddy mudslingers
- [ ] Two witches
- [ ] A pyramid sandcastle
- [ ] A mermaid
- [ ] A wooden mallet
- [ ] A man with his feet in stocks
- [ ] Two tipped cauldrons
- [ ] A flag with eight faces
- [ ] Two bent swords
- [ ] Three flattened knights
- [ ] A globe
- [ ] Cave clothes hung out to dry
- [ ] A fire-breathing gargoyle
- [ ] A skipping monster

HERE ARE SOME ANSWERS TO THE HARDEST PUZZLES. DON'T GIVE UP ON THE OTHERS – WHY NOT ASK YOUR FRIENDS TO HELP?

GREAT GUIDEBOOKS

CAVE LIFE QUIZ

1. Tools were made of stone 2. Hunted and gathered food
3. Paintings of animals 4. Bears & Lions 5. Elephants
6. Rhinos & Mammoths 7. Fire 8. Pig 9. Clothes & Tools
10. Spears

BUILDING BLOCKS

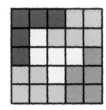 

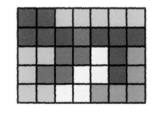 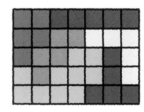

SCALING LADDERS

WALL → **F**ALL → FE**L**L → FEE**L**
BOTTLE → B**A**TTLE → **C**ATTLE → CA**S**TLE

RIGHT-ANGLED ANIMALS

WRITE LIKE AN EGYPTIAN

Top: Find a crocodile face! Find another crocodile elsewhere in this book! Don't take your time, make it snappy! Middle: Also look for a secret drawing on a stone wall. Clue: it is not on this page and is lit by fire.

First published 2016 by Walker Books Ltd, 87 Vauxhall Walk, London SE11 5HJ • 2 4 6 8 10 9 7 5 3 1 • © 1987–2016 Martin Handford • The right of Martin Handford to be identified as author/illustrator of this work has been asserted by him in accordance with the Copyright, Designs and Patents Act 1988. • This book has been typeset in Wallyfont and Optima • Printed in China • All rights reserved. • British Library Cataloguing in Publication Data: a catalogue record for this book is available from the British Library. • ISBN 978-1-4063-6819-2 • www.walker.co.uk

ONE LAST THING...

Did you find a shield with Wally's red-and-white bobble hat? And did you find another with Odlaw's yellow-and-black bobble hat? Keep searching!